TRUE
SERENITY

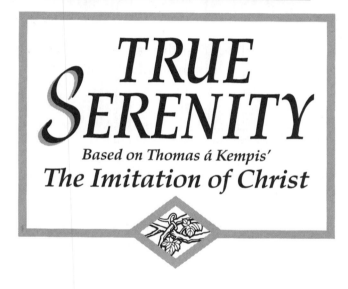

TRUE SERENITY

Based on Thomas á Kempis'
The Imitation of Christ

AVE MARIA PRESS   Notre Dame, Indiana 46556

John Kirvan is an experienced author and editor of religious books. He currently lives in southern California.

The passages of *The Imitation of Christ* included in this book are free adaptations made from the classic English translation by Richard Whitford first published about 1530.

Copyright © 1995 Quest Associates

International Standard Book Number: 0-87793-562-9

Library of Congress Card Number: 95-77234

Cover and text design by Elizabeth J. French

Printed and bound in the United States of America

Contents

My friend, hear my words.
They are of surpassing sweetness,
and exceed all learning of the philosophers
and wise men of this world.
My words are spirit and life,
not to be weighed by human understanding.
They are not to be quoted for vain pleasure,
but are to be heard in silence.

The Imitation of Christ

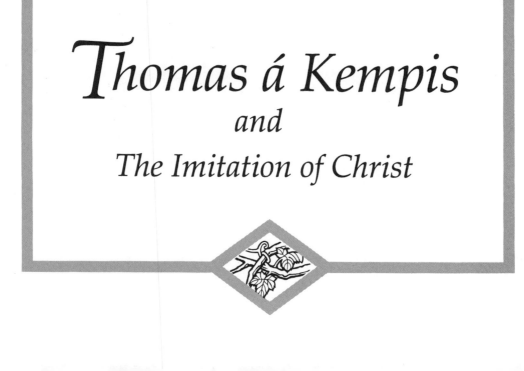

Thomas á Kempis
and
The Imitation of Christ

No one really knows whether Thomas á Kempis, a Flemish monk of the 15th century, wrote *The Imitation of Christ* or whether he just copied an existing manuscript.

But it doesn't really matter. Whoever wrote it created a work that was almost instantly recognized as a spiritual masterpiece. Five centuries and hundreds of editions in dozens of languages after its original publication, it is still one of the world's most read books. There have been at least five hundred editions in English since Richard Whitford published his translation about 1530, the translation on which this book is based. There are at least a dozen English versions in print at this moment.

Its readership from the beginning has stretched far beyond the cloistered readers for whom it was first intended. Its appreciative readership runs from Thomas More, who included it in his short list of three Christian books that everyone should read, through Samuel Johnson and Thomas Carlyle to George Eliot, who confessed, "it makes one long to be a saint for a few months. Verily its piety has its foundations in the depth of the divine-human soul."

But in our own times, we must admit, many have never even heard of *The Imitation of Christ* and many others have relegated it to history as propagating a spirituality that is out of date and out of touch.

Two things have conspired to produce this reaction.

The first is our response to its language of self-denial and "world-hatred." Contemporary theology stresses a world so beloved of God that God sent his only Son to live and die in and for it. It urges and even commands us to love the world and work to fulfill its creator-given destiny. In such a context "self-denial" seems perilously close to "self-hatred," a denial of the Incarnation. "World-hatred" seems like an invitation to escape the harsh realities of daily living and our responsibility to the planet and the millions who inhabit it.

But we know instinctively and profoundly that the world á Kempis warns us about and the world we are meant to love, serve, and nourish are far from the same thing. Only the word is the same.

We are to be the stewards of the world given to every generation of humankind to nourish our bodies and souls with its beauty and its plenty, the world so much loved by its creator, the world to which he gave his Son, the incarnational context of our lives.

But we know only too well that there is another reality which we also call "the world"—a spirit, a set of standards that threatens always to permeate the days of our lives, how we earn our living, raise our families, and make the hundreds of daily decisions about what is right and what is wrong. This is the "world" that is too much with us, that insists that nothing is real that cannot be measured and weighed, the "world" where self-interest is a virtue, the "world" of beckoning greed and crime, of common, petty evil that impinges on our lives relentlessly, the "world" that seeks to define us. It is about the lure of this "world" that the Lord of á Kempis warns us.

However similar the language, we know the difference.

The second thing that lessens the appeal of á Kempis in our days is the dominance of modern "ego support" psychology in our search for meaning. We have grown up with its process, its techniques, its values, and the language in which they are stated. The values of modern psychology are in explicit contrast, even conflict, with the world of á Kempis. An unending stream of self-help books comes up against a book that says in the end, at the deepest level of our being, only God can help. "Self-fulfillment" clashes with "self-surrender."

We have gotten used to a life centered on a search for self. To read á Kempis is to be challenged to turn that world inside out, upside down. Our search for self, he insists, must give way to a search for God, in whom alone, we are promised, we will finally find our self.

Given our recent theological and psychological history it is not a message that is easy to hear. But given the spiritual hunger we are experiencing, it may just be possible to overcome our first reactions to find the classical spiritual nourishment that á Kempis offers.

This "journey" has been created to give you a taste of *The Imitation of Christ* that remains faithful to the flavor of the whole, much longer work.

You will discover here a spiritual world that emphasizes the intimate relationship of the Lord with those who approach him. These morning meditations edited from the text of *The Imitation* are conversations between the Lord and his "friend," the seeker after spiritual truth. The reference (e.g., 3:1) at the end of each selection indicates the book and the chapter in the original from which the passage has been taken.

A second theme runs through the meditation passages. It is God's promise of everlasting, true peace and rest to anyone who loves and serves him. The cost of this peace will be to put God above everything else, above the "world," above self. Any other peace is illusory, any other price is not enough.

Here then is a gateway to the spiritual wisdom of Thomas á Kempis, a concentrated, systematic experience of one of the great spiritual masters of the Christian era.

Join millions of others who over five centuries have found in the wisdom and words of á Kempis an invitation to union with God that is hard to resist, and a wise support in the journey.

How to Pray This Book

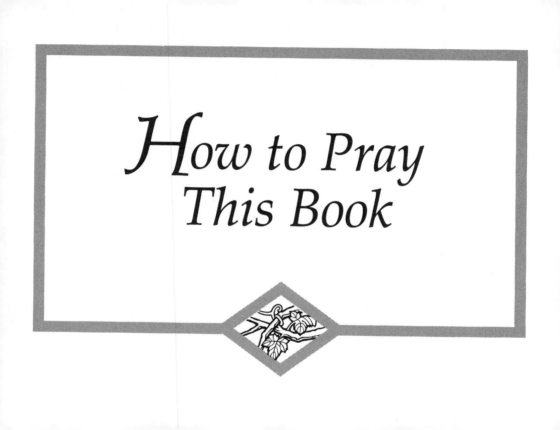

The purpose of this book is to open a gate for you, to make accessible one of the world's great spiritual masterpieces, *The Imitation of Christ*, and the spiritual experience and wisdom of its writer, Thomas á Kempis.

This is not a book for mere reading. It invites you to meditate and pray its words on a daily basis over a period of thirty days.

It is a handbook for a spiritual journey.

Before you read the "rules" for taking this spiritual journey, remember that this book is meant to free your spirit, not confine it. If on any day the meditation does not resonate well for you, turn elsewhere to find a passage which seems to best fit the spirit of your day and your soul. Don't hesitate to repeat a day as often as you like until you feel that you have discovered what the Spirit, through the words of the author, has to say to your spirit.

Here are suggestions on one way to use this book as a cornerstone of your prayers.

As Your Day Begins

As the day begins set aside a quiet moment in a quiet place to read the meditation suggested for the day.

The passage is short. It never runs more than a couple of hundred words, but it has been carefully selected to give a spiritual focus, a spiritual center to your whole day. It is designed to remind you as another day begins of your own existence at a spiritual level. It is meant to put you in the presence of the spiritual master who is your companion and teacher on this journey. But most of all the purpose of the passage is to remind you that at this moment and at every moment during this day you will be living and acting in the presence of a God who invites you continually, but quietly to live in and through him.

A word of advice: read slowly. Very slowly. The meditation has been broken down into sense lines to help you do just this. Don't read to get to the end, but to savor each part of the meditation. You never know what short phrase, what word, will trigger a response in your spirit. Give the words a chance. After all you are not just reading this passage, you are praying it. You are establishing a mood of serenity for your whole day. What's the rush?

All Through Your Day

Immediately following the day's reading you will find a single sentence which we call a mantra, a word borrowed from the Hindu tradition.

This phrase is meant as a companion for your spirit as it moves through a busy day. Write it down on a 3″ x 5″ card or on the appropriate page of your daybook. Look at it as often as you can. Repeat it quietly to yourself and go on your way.

It is not meant to stop you in your tracks or to distract you from responsibilities, but simply, gently to remind you of the presence of God and your desire to respond to this presence.

As Your Day Is Ending

This is a time for letting go of the day.

Find a quiet place and quiet your spirit. Breathe deeply. Inhale, exhale—slowly and deliberately, again and again until you feel your body let go of its tension.

Now read the evening prayer slowly, phrase by phrase. You may recognize at once that we have taken one of the most familiar evening prayers of the Christian tradition and woven into it phrases taken from the meditation with which you began your day and the mantra that has accompanied you all through your day. In this way a simple evening prayer gathers together the spiritual character of the day that is now ending as it began—in the presence of God.

It is a time for summary and closure.

Invite God to embrace you with love and to protect you through the night.

Sleep well.

Some Other Ways to Use This Book

1. Use it anyway your spirit suggests. As mentioned earlier, skip a passage that doesn't resonate for you on a given day, or repeat for a second day or even several days a passage whose richness speaks to you. The truths of a spiritual life are not absorbed in a

day, or for that matter, in a lifetime. So take your time. Be patient with the Lord. Be patient with yourself.

2. Take two passages and/or their mantras—the more contrasting the better—and "bang" them together. Spend time discovering how their similarities or differences illumine your path.

3. Start a spiritual journal to record and deepen your experience of this thirty-day journey. Using either the mantra or another phrase from the reading that appeals to you, write a spiritual account of your day, a spiritual reflection. Create your own meditation.

4. Join the millions who are seeking to deepen their spiritual life by joining with others to form small groups. More and more people are doing just this to aid and support each other in their mutual quest. Meet once a week, or at least every other week to

discuss and pray about one of the meditations. There are lots of books and guides available to help you make such a group effective.

Thirty Days with
Thomas á Kempis

Day One

◆◆◆◆◆

My Day Begins

I shall take heed, says the devout soul,
and I shall hear what my Lord Jesus shall speak in me.

Blessed are they that hear Jesus speaking in their soul,
and who take from his mouth
some word of comfort.

Blessed be those ears that hear
the secret whisperings of Jesus
and heed not the deceitful whisperings of this world;

and blessed be the good plain ears
that heed not the world's wisdom,
but rather take heed
to what God speaks and teaches in the soul.

Blessed be those eyes that are closed to outward vanities,
and that take heed to the inward movings of God.

Blessed be they also that grow in virtue
and daily perform
the corporal and spiritual works of mercy.
They shall receive daily more and more
the secret inspirations and inward teachings of God.

And blessed be they who commit themselves wholly
to serve God, and for his service
put away all hindrances of the world.

O you my soul!
Take heed to that which has been said before
and shut the door of your soul to the world
that you may hear spiritually what our Lord Jesus
speaks fully in your soul.

Thus says my Beloved:
"I am your health, I am your peace. I am your life.
Keep me at your side and you shall find peace in me;
forsake the love of transitory things
and seek things that are everlasting" (3:1).

All Through the Day

You are my health, my peace,
and my life.

My Day Is Ending

O Lord,
you have been with me all through the day.
Now evening has come.
The shadows have lengthened into darkness.
Let my busy world now grow quiet,
the feverish concerns of this day be stilled,
my work put away.
Grant me a night of silence with you.

I have sought all through the day
to hear your whisperings in my soul
and to close my ears to the clear call of the world.

Let me abandon all that passes with the day.
Let me choose you.
Stay by my side and speak to my spirit
as I seek what will last forever.
Be my health. Be my peace. Be my life.

And as my day ends
keep me in your embrace through the night,
give me quiet rest and your peace,
now and forever.
Amen.

Day Two

My Day Begins

My friend, let go of yourself and you will find me.

If you wholly give yourself into my hands
and take nothing back
you shall have me.

Some persons surrender themselves to me,
but they hold something back.
They do not trust me fully,
and go on trying to provide for themselves.

Others, at the beginning,
offer all of themselves to me,
but when a difficult time comes
they put their trust back in themselves.

Such persons will never know perfect peace
and freedom of heart.

Give all for all
and hold back nothing.

Stand purely and strongly and steadfastly in me
and you shall have me.
You shall be so free in heart and in soul
that darkness shall never have power over you.

Seek out—study—pray for this freedom of spirit
that I speak of.

Seek always in your heart
to be free of everything that binds you,
that in love you may die to yourself
and to all worldly things
and blessedly live to me.

If you do this
all unimportant questions
shall fail and fade and go away.
Crippling fear and misplaced love shall die in you.
You shall live in me and I in you (3-37).

All Through the Day

Let go of yourself
and you will find me.

My Day Is Ending

O Lord,
you have been with me all through the day.
Now evening has come.
The shadows have lengthened into darkness.
Let my busy world now grow quiet,
the feverish concerns of my day be stilled,
my work put away.
Reward me with your silence.

O Lord, all through the day
I have heard your invitation to let go of myself.
It is so easy to say that I will surrender myself to you
and give you all for all.
But I can think of a thousand things

that I would find easier to hold back,
a thousand ways in which to hold onto myself.
Take away my crippling fears of surrender to you.
And as my day ends,
keep me in your embrace through the night,
give me quiet rest and your peace,
now and forever.
Amen.

Day Three

My Day Begins

My friend,
be not grieved,
though you see others honored and exalted,
and yourself forgotten.
If you will raise up your heart to me in heaven,
these small slights will not grieve you.

O Lord,
we live in great darkness

and are easily deceived by the values of this world.
But truthfully,
if I look at myself closely, I should see
that there was never real wrong done to me
by any creature;
I have nothing to complain of.

I have often sinned and
deeply offended you, and my brothers and sisters.

To me, therefore is due sorrow;
to you honor, praise, and glory.

And I know that unless I can bring myself to the point
where I gladly accept being forsaken
and very unimportant by the standards of the world,

I will never know inward peace
and never be spiritually illumined,
never made fully one with you (3:41).

All Through the Day

I know true peace only
when I am one with you.

My Day Is Ending

O Lord you have been with me all through the day.
Now evening has come.
The shadows have lengthened into darkness.
Let my busy world now grow quiet,
the feverish concerns of my day be stilled,
my work put away.
Reward me with your silence.

All through the day
I have tried to remember how often and how easily
I have offended my brothers and my sisters,
and how little I have to complain of
in their treatment of me.
But in truth,

I am not yet ready to welcome
being thought of as unimportant by the world.
Until then, I know, I will not have earned your peace.

But as this day ends I ask of you O Lord:
keep me in your embrace through the night,
give me quiet rest and your peace,
now and forever.
Amen.

Day Four

My Day Begins

My friend,
I am he who alone can teach you wisdom
and give you more understanding
than can be given by human learning.

Anyone to whom I shall speak
will soon be made wise
and profit greatly in their spirit.

Disappointment shall be the lot

of those who seek wisdom only out of curiosity
taking no heed of the way to serve me.

My friend,
let not the world's fair and subtle words move you,
for the kingdom of heaven lives not in their words
but in virtuous works.

Take heed rather to my words
for they will inflame your heart
and enlighten your understanding.
They will bring compunction to your heart for sins past,
and will often cause great heavenly comfort
suddenly to come into your soul.

Do not read and study just to be thought wise,
but rather to still the world in your spirit

and to hear more clearly my voice.

This shall be more profitable to you
than the knowledge of many difficult and subtle questions.

When you have read widely and learned much,
it still behooves you
to come to one who is the beginning of all things,
that is God alone,
or your knowledge shall little avail you (3:43).

All Through the Day

Without you all my other
knowledge means very little.

My Day Is Ending

O Lord,
you have been with me all through the day.
Now evening has come.
The shadows have lengthened into darkness.
Let my busy world now grow quiet,
the feverish concerns of my day be stilled,
my work put away.
Grant me a night of silence with you.

Let me understand and accept
that it is not in the world's kind words
that I shall find life and peace,
but only in your words.

Inflame my heart and enlighten my understanding.

Bring sorrow to my heart for the sins of my life
and comfort to my soul.
Let the only wisdom I seek
be yours, O Lord.

For now,
keep me in your embrace through the night,
give me quiet rest
and your peace,
now and forever.
Amen.

Day Five

◆◆◆◆◆

My Day Begins

Some persons,
my friend,
through the inward love they have for me,
have learned many great things
and are able to speak truly and beautifully
of the high mysteries
of my Godhead.

But even they profit more
in forsaking all things for my sake

than in studying for high and subtle learning.

For I speak to everyone.

To some I speak of common things,
to others special things,
to still others I appear gently
in signs and figures,
and to some
I give great understanding of scripture
and open to them great mysteries.

Everyone of them reads the same words,
but each hears differently,
hears what is meant for them.

For I am within,
living in every word you shall hear and read.

For all
I am the teacher of truth,
the searcher of the heart,
the knower of thoughts,
the promoter of good works,
and the rewarder of all.

Hear my words (3:43).

All Through the Day

You are alive in every word I read or hear.

My Day Is Ending

O Lord,
you have been with me all through the day.
Now evening has come.
The shadows have lengthened into darkness.
Let my busy world now grow quiet,
the feverish concerns of my day be stilled,
my work put away.

Let the words you have spoken to my spirit today
continue to grow within me even as I rest.
Help me to understand them.
You alone are the source of truth.

You know what is in my heart and in my thoughts.
You who are within every word I hear or read,
hear now the words of my heart.
Hear the words my silent spirit speaks.

Grant me a night of silence with you.
Keep me in your embrace through the night,
give me quiet rest
and your peace,
now and forever.
Amen.

Day Six

◆◆◆◆◆

My Day Begins

Now, my friend,
I shall teach you the very true way of peace
and perfect liberty.

Learn to fulfill another's will rather than your own.

Choose always the lowest place
and desire to be under others rather than above.

Choose always to have little worldly riches
rather than much.

Desire always and pray
that the will of God be wholly done in you.

Such a person will enter into
the way of true peace and inward serenity.

My Lord,
this short lesson that you have taught me,
is in itself perfection.
It is short in words, but it is full of wisdom
and the ways of virtue.
If I keep it fully and faithfully,
my spirit will not again be so frequently restless.
For whenever my soul is restless and discontented
it is because I have departed from this lesson
and from your teachings.
But you, Lord Jesus,

who have all things in your power
and my welfare in your hands
increase your grace in me
that I may henceforth fulfill these teachings,
and that I do
whatever may bring honor to you
and health to my soul. (3:23).

All Through the Day

Let the will of God
be done fully in me.

My Day Is Ending

O Lord,
you have been with me all through the day.
Now evening has come.
The shadows have lengthened into darkness.
Let my busy world now grow quiet,
the feverish concerns of my day be stilled,
my work put away.

Let me know your will for me,
but most of all give my soul the strength
to follow you in all things.
It is not easy for me
to seek less of the world's riches than more,
to seek the lowest rather than the highest places

in the judgment of the world.
But only in this way
can I achieve true peace and serenity of spirit.

Grant me a night of silence with you.
Keep me in your embrace through the night,
give me quiet rest
and your peace,
now and forever.
Amen.

Day Seven

◆◆◆◆◆

My Day Begins

My friend,
you shall never be safe from temptation
and tribulation in this life.
Therefore you will need to protect your spirit
as long as you live.
For you live and walk among spiritual enemies
who will trouble and vex you from every side;
Unless you use at all times
and in all places the shield of patience,
your spirit shall very soon be wounded.

And beyond this,
if you do not fix your spirit firmly in me,
prepared to suffer all things patiently for me,
you will not be able to sustain your spiritual ardor
and know the rewards of the saints.

If you seek rest in this life,
how can you expect everlasting rest?
Seek here not rest, but patience,
and seek true rest, not on earth, but in heaven,
not in other creatures, but in God only,
in whom alone it is found.

To enjoy the love of God you must suffer gladly all things:
all labors, sorrows, temptations, vexations,
all anguish, neediness, sickness, injuries,
evil sayings, humiliations,

all oppressions, confusions, and corrections.
These bring a person to virtue,
these prove who are my true imitators
and make them ready for a heavenly reward.
I shall give to such a soul
an everlasting reward for its short labor,
and infinite glory for its passing pain.
Wait patiently for my coming.
Do willingly my bidding, accept my comfort.
Trust in me.
Do not abandon my service
because of pain or out of fear,
but employ your body and soul constantly to my honor.
I will be with you
and help you in every trouble that comes to you.
So may it be (3-35).

All Through the Day

I am with you and help you
in every trouble.

My Day Is Ending

O Lord,
you have been with me all through the day.
Now evening has come.
The shadows have lengthened into darkness.
Let my busy world now grow quiet,
the feverish concerns of my day be stilled,
my work put away,
and patience grow within my spirit.

And as I prepare to close my eyes,
grant me rest from the labors, sorrows, and temptations
—the anguish and confusions of the day.
Grant me for these few hours

a taste of the eternal rest that you promise
to those who seek only you in this life.
Hold back the sufferings of the day.

Grant me a night of silence with you.
Keep me in your embrace through the night,
give me quiet rest
and your peace,
now and forever.
Amen.

Day Eight

My Day Begins

The faults we cannot overcome in ourselves and others
we must patiently suffer until
our good Lord otherwise disposes.

Work today, therefore, and always
to be patient with the failings of others,
for you have many things in yourself
that others must endure.

If you cannot become the person you want to be,
how can you expect perfection in others?

We would gladly have others perfect,
but we will not amend our own lives.

We would like others to be corrected immediately
for their failings,
but we resist correction.

We resent the freedom of others,
but we will not be denied anything we desire.

It is evident that we seldom think of our neighbor
as we do of ourselves.

God has ordained that each one of us
shall learn to bear another's burden.
For in this world no one is without faults,

no one is without burdens,
and no one is totally wise.

It is for each of us
not to judge others
but rather
to bear their burden,
to comfort them,
to help them,
to counsel them (1:16).

All Through the Day

If I cannot be the person I want to be,
how can I demand perfection in others?

My Day Is Ending

O Lord,
you have been with me all through the day.
Now evening has come.
The shadows have lengthened into darkness.
Let my busy world now grow quiet,
the feverish concerns of my day be stilled,
my work put away.
For this one moment let me think of others
rather than just myself.
They too desire the peace and serenity for which I pray.
Be patient with them
and grant that I may not judge them,

but willingly bear their burdens.
Teach me to reach out to them
as you reach out to me,
to comfort and help them.

Grant to us all a night of silence with you.
Embrace us,
give us quiet rest
and your peace,
now and forever.
Amen.

Day Nine

My Day Begins

Speak Lord, for I am ready to hear you.

I am your servant: give me wisdom and understanding
to know your commandments.
Bend my heart to follow your holy teachings,
that they may seep into my soul.

The children of Israel said to Moses:
"Speak to us and we shall hear you;
but let not our God speak directly to us,

lest we die of fear."
Rather, I ask meekly, with Samuel the prophet,
that you speak to me directly,
and I shall gladly hear you.

Lord you are the inward inspirer
and giver of light to all prophets,
for you alone can fully inform me and instruct me.
Without you their words profit me little.

Your prophets speak wisely,
but you give me the spirit to understand them.
They speak truly,
but you provide fire to kindle them in my heart.
They speak words,
but you declare the sentence.

They describe great mysteries,
but you provide the understanding.
Let me hear your word and do it,
know your word and love it,
believe your word and fulfill it.

Speak therefore directly to me,
for I am your servant
and I am ready to hear you.
You have the words of eternal life,
speak them to me.
To you let there be joy,
honor, and glory everlasting (3:2).

All Through the Day

Speak Lord, for I am ready to hear you.

My Day Is Ending

O Lord,
you have been with me all through the day.
Now evening has come.
The shadows have lengthened into darkness.
Let my busy world now grow quiet,
the feverish concerns of my day be stilled,
my work put away.

All through the day I have asked you to speak to me,
and told you that I was ready to hear your words.
Kindle those words in my soul.
Give them life.
Give me the spirit of understanding.
Hearing your word let me live it,

knowing your word let me love it,
believing your word let it be fulfilled in me.

Grant me now a night of silence with you.
Keep me in your embrace through the night,
give me quiet rest
and your peace,
now and forever.
Amen.

Day Ten

◆◆◆◆◆

My Day Begins

Love is a great and good thing,
and alone makes heavy burdens light.
It balances what is pleasing with what is displeasing.
It bears heavy burdens and feels them not.
It makes bitter things savory and sweet.

The noble love of Jesus,
perfectly imprinted in our soul,
makes us do great things
and stirs us always to seek perfection

and to grow more and more in grace and goodness.
Love will always bring our mind upward to God
and will not be occupied with things of the world.

Spiritual love is free from all worldly affections,
so that the inward sight of our soul is not darkened,
and our affection for heavenly things,
our liberty of soul,
is not upset by either great losses or gains
in our daily life.

Nothing therefore is sweeter than love,
nothing higher, nothing stronger, nothing larger,
nothing more joyful, nothing fuller,
and nothing better in heaven or on earth.

For love descends from God,

and may not rest finally in anything less than God.

A lover of God flies high, runs swiftly, is merry in God,
is free in soul, gives all for all and has all in all,
rests in one high goodness above all things,
from whom all goodness flows and proceeds.

The lover of God beholds not only the gift,
but the giver above all gifts (3:5).

All Through the Day

All love descends from God.

My Day Is Ending

O Lord,
you have been with me all through the day.
Now evening has come.
The shadows have lengthened into darkness.
Let my busy world now grow quiet,
the feverish concerns of my day be stilled,
my work put away.

Let me quietly contemplate your love
for nothing is stronger or more joyful.
Nothing on earth or in heaven is better.
Let me know the freedom of soul your love brings.
Let your love descend upon me.
Raise up my soul to you.

Fill the night's silence with your love.
Be present to me.

Keep me in your embrace through the night,
give me quiet rest
and your peace,
now and forever.
Amen.

Day Eleven

◆◆◆◆

My Day Begins

Love knows no measure
but is fervent without measure.
It feels no burden, it shirks no labor.
It desires more than it may attain.
It complains of no impossibility, for it thinks
that all things may be done for its beloved.
Love therefore does many great things
and brings them to completion,
whereas the one who is not a lover faints and fails.

Love wakes much and sleeps little,
and sleeping sleeps not.
Love faints, but is not weary,
is restrained in its liberty, and yet knows great freedom.
It sees reasons to be afraid, and fears not.
Like a quick brand or spark of fire,
it flames always upwards by fervor of love unto God,
and through the special help of grace
is delivered from all perils and dangers.

The spiritual lover knows what it is to say:
you, Lord God, are my whole love and desire.
You are all mine and I am all yours.
Gather my heart into your love that I may know
how sweet it is to serve you,
and how joyful it is to please you.

I shall sing to you the song of love.
I shall follow you, my beloved,
wheresoever you go,
and my soul shall never be too weary to praise you
with the joyful song of spiritual love
that I shall sing to you.

I shall love you more than myself
and myself for you.
I shall love all others in you and for you,
as the law of love commands
which is given by you (3:5).

All Through the Day

Love knows no measure.

My Day Is Ending

O Lord,
you have been with me all through the day.
Now evening has come.
The shadows have lengthened into darkness.
Let my busy world now grow quiet,
the feverish concerns of my day be stilled,
my work put away.

You, Lord God,
are to be my whole love and desire.
You are all mine and I am all yours.
Gather my heart into your love that I may know
how sweet it is to serve you,

and how joyful it is to please you.
I desire to love you more than myself
and myself for you.
I desire to love all others in you and for you.

Grant me now a moment of silence with you.
Embrace me
through the night with your sleepless love,
give me quiet rest
and your peace,
now and forever.
Amen.

Day Twelve

◆◆◆◆◆

My Day Begins

Blessed be you, heavenly Father,
the Father of my Lord Jesus Christ,
for you have vouchsafed to remember me,
and to comfort me with your gracious presence.
I bless you and glorify you always,
with your only begotten Son and the Holy Spirit,
without ending.
O my Lord God, most faithful lover,
when you come into my heart,

all that is within me is joy.
You are my glory and the joy of my heart,
my hope and my whole refuge in all my troubles.

Teach me, heavenly Father, a love that is
swift, pure, meek, joyous and glad,
strong, patient, faithful,
wise, forbearing, fatherly,
and never self-seeking;
for whenever we seek ourselves we fall from love.

Teach me a love that is
circumspect, righteous,
not weak, not fragile, not attached to vanities,
sober, chaste, stable, quiet, and wise.
And inasmuch as I am yet feeble in love
and imperfect in virtue,

I need your constant comfort and help.

Visit me often therefore,
and instruct me with your holy teachings.

Make me ready and able to love you,
strong to suffer for you,
and stable to persevere in you (3:5).

All Through the Day

You are making me ready and able
to love you.

My Day Is Ending

O Lord,
you have been with me all through the day.
Now evening has come.
The shadows have lengthened into darkness.
Let my busy world grow quiet,
the feverish concerns of my day be stilled,
my work put away.

And inasmuch as I am so weak in my love
and so imperfect in virtue,
I need much comfort and help from you.
Visit me through the night
and teach me the truth of your love even as I sleep.
Make me ready and able to love you,

strong enough to suffer for your love,
and faithful to the end.

Grant me now a moment of silence with you.
Keep me in your embrace through the night,
give me quiet rest
and your peace,
now and forever.
Amen.

Day Thirteen

◆◆◆◆◆

My Day Begins

My friend, says our Savior Christ,
here is how you should pray for what you desire:

Lord if it be your will, be it done as I ask;
and if it be to your praise, be it fulfilled in your name.
And if you see it good and profitable to me,
give me grace to use it in your honor.
But if you know it to be harmful to me
then take from me such desire.

Every desire does not come from the Holy Spirit
even though it may seem right and good,
for it is sometimes very difficult to judge
whether a good spirit or an evil one
is behind this or that desire;
or whether you are being moved
only of your own spirit.
Many are deceived in the end
who first seem to have been moved
by the Holy Spirit.

Therefore, with fear of God
and with meekness of heart,
you should desire and ask
whatever comes to your mind,
and forsaking yourself completely

commit all things to God and say:

Lord you know what is best for me.
Give me what you will,
as much as you will,
and when you will.
Do with me as you know best,
as it most pleases you,
and as is most to your honor.

I am your creature and in your hands.
Lead me where you will.
I am your servant, ready to do all things
that you command,
for I desire not to live to myself but to you (3:15).

All Through the Day

You, Lord, know what is best for me.

My Day Is Ending

O Lord,
you have been with me all through the day.
Now evening has come.
The shadows have lengthened into darkness.
Let my busy world grow quiet,
the feverish concerns of my day be stilled,
my work put away.

Lord you know what is best for me.
Give me only what you will, when you will.
Do with me as you know best,
as it most pleases you, and is most to your honor.
I am your creation and I rest in your hands.
Lead me where you will.

I am your servant;
I desire to live not for myself but for you alone.

Grant me now a moment of silence with you.
Keep me in your embrace through the night,
give me quiet rest
and your peace,
now and forever.
Amen.

Day Fourteen

My Day Begins

Kindest Lord Jesus,
grant me your grace,
that it may always be with me,
and work with me
and persevere with me unto the end.

Grant that I may always desire and will
that which is most pleasing
and most acceptable to you.

Let your will be my will.
And let my will always follow your will.

Let my will and desire be united with you,
and grant that I will never choose anything
but your will.
Grant me that I might die
to all worldly things
and that I may love to be overlooked
and to be someone unknown in this world.

Grant me also,
above all things that can be desired,
that I may rest in you,
and fully know peace of heart.
For you Lord are the only true peace of heart,

the only perfect serenity of body and soul,
and without you
all things are sad and without true rest.
Amen (3:5).

All Through the Day

Only in you is there perfect serenity.

My Day Is Ending

O Lord,
you have been with me all through the day.
Now evening has come.
The shadows have lengthened into darkness.
Let my busy world grow quiet,
the feverish concerns of my day be stilled,
my work put away.

Kindest Lord Jesus
grant me your grace
that it may always be with me.
and work with me,
and stay with me to the end.

Grant that I may always desire and choose
that which is most pleasing
and acceptable to you.

Grant me now a moment of silence.
Keep me in your embrace through the night,
give me quiet rest
and your peace,
now and forever.
Amen.

Day Fifteen

◆◆◆◆

My Day Begins

My friend, says the Lord to his servant,
allow me to do with you what I will,
for I know what is best and most expedient for you.
You use human reason, and are moved too easily
by your affections and the world's opinions
and so you often err and are deceived.

Lord, it is true as you say:
your providence is much better for me
than all I can do or say for myself.

It is true that we are very shaky
when we do not trust wholly in you.
Therefore Lord, as long as my spirit
remains steadfast and stable,
do with me as it pleases you,
for it will be only for my good.

Whether you come to me in darkness or light,
I will bless you.
Whether you choose to comfort me,
or to let me live without all comfort,
I bless you equally.

My friend, says the Lord, I choose to be with you.
If you will walk with me,
you must be prepared
for suffering as well as joy,

and as happy to be needy and poor
as wealthy and rich.

Lord,
I will gladly suffer for you whatever befalls me.
With equal gratitude I will accept from your hand
good and bad, bitter and sweet, gladness and sorrow,
and for all things that befall me
with all my heart I will thank you.

Only keep me from sin, my Lord,
and I shall dread neither death nor hell.
Remove not my name out of the book of life,
and whatsoever shall befall me,
shall not cause me sorrow (3:17).

All Through the Day

In darkness or in light I thank you.

My Day Is Ending

O Lord,
you have been with me all through the day.
Now evening has come.
The shadows have lengthened into darkness.
Let my busy world grow quiet,
the feverish concerns of my day be stilled,
my work put away.

In spiritual darkness or in light,
by day or by night,
let me always bless you.
Whether you choose to comfort me
or to let me live without your comfort,
let me bless you equally.

Do with me as it pleases you
for it will be only for my good.

Grant me now a moment of silence.
Keep me in your embrace through the night,
give me quiet rest
and your peace,
now and forever.
Amen.

Day Sixteen

◆◆◆◆

My Day Begins

My friend,
why do you complain?
Consider my passion and the sufferings of my saints,
and you shall see that you suffer very little.
Remember how greatly others have suffered
in my name so that you may the more easily
bear your little griefs.
But whether your sufferings be great or little,
learn to bear them with patience.

The more you learn patience the wiser you shall be,
the more merit you shall have,
and the lighter will be your burden.

The patient soul,
whenever any adversity or wrong comes its way,
no matter from whom or what it may be,
or how often,
receives it thankfully,
as though it came from the hand of God,
and considers it a rich gift and a great blessing.
For we know that there is nothing
that we might suffer
that need pass without great merit.

Be ready therefore to do battle if you seek victory.

Without battle you will not achieve the crown of patience.
Resist strongly and suffer patiently.
For without labor no one can come to rest,
and without battle no one achieves victory.

O Lord Jesus,
make possible to me by grace
that which is not possible to me by nature.
You know well that I suffer very little
and that I am easily cast down by the smallest adversity.
Therefore, I pray that trouble and adversity
may hereafter, for your sake and in your name,
be welcomed by me,
for truly to suffer and be vexed for you is very good
and profitable for the health of my soul (3:19).

All Through the Day

My burden is light.

My Day Is Ending

O Lord,
you have been with me all through the day.
Now evening has come.
The shadows have lengthened into darkness.
Let my busy world grow quiet,
the feverish concerns of my day be stilled,
my work put away.

You have, Lord, taken this day to remind me
that without labor there is no rest,
without battle there is no victory.
Make possible to me, Lord Jesus, by your grace
that which seems impossible to me by nature.

It takes very little, the smallest adversity
to discourage me.
Let me by your grace,
begin again tomorrow.

But for now grant me a moment of your silence.
Keep me in your embrace through the night,
give me quiet rest
and your peace,
now and forever.
Amen.

Day Seventeen

◆◆◆◆◆

My Day Begins

My friend,
above all things and in all things,
rest your soul in your Lord God,
for God is the eternal rest of all angels and saints.

Give me Lord Jesus,
special grace to rest in you above all creatures,
above all health and fairness,
above all honor and glory,
above all dignity and power,

above all wisdom and policy,
above all riches and crafts,
above all gladness of body and soul,
above all fame and praising,
above all sweetness and consolation,
above all hope and promise,
above all merit and desire,
above all gifts and rewards that you might send me,
and above all joy and mirth
that my heart might take or feel.
And also above all angels and archangels
and all the company of heavenly spirits,
above all things visible and invisible,
and above all things that are not you.

Above all things and in all things,
let me rest my soul in you, my Lord God,
for you alone
are our eternal rest (3:31).

All Through the Day

Put nothing above me in your heart.

My Day Is Ending

O Lord,
you have been with me all through the day.
Now evening has come.
The shadows have lengthened into darkness.
Let my busy world grow quiet,
the feverish concerns of my day be stilled,
my work put away.

Let me rest my soul in you, Lord,
for you are the eternal rest of all angels and saints.
Give me, Lord Jesus,
the special grace to rest in you
above all creatures,

above all things visible and invisible,
and above all and anything
that is not you.

Grant me a moment of your silence.
Keep me in your embrace through the night,
give me quiet rest
and your peace,
now and forever.
Amen.

Day Eighteen

My Day Begins

O my Lord Jesus Christ,
most loving spouse, most pure lover and
governor of every creature,
give me wings of perfect liberty
that I might fly high and rest in you.

When shall I finally give you my full attention
and see and feel how sweet you are?

When shall I give you all of myself so perfectly

that I shall not be aware of myself but of you only?

When shall you visit me
as you visit your true lovers?

Now I am often sad
and complain about the miseries of this life,
and with sorrow and great heaviness of heart bear them.
For many hard things happen daily in my life
which trouble me constantly
and darken my understanding.
They hinder me and distract my soul away from you,
They so burden me that I lose my peace of mind
and my desire for you.
I beseech you Lord,
that the sighs of my heart
and my inward desires,

my many troubles,
may somehow move you
to incline your ear to hear my prayers (3:21).

All Through the Day

When shall I finally give you
my full attention?

My Day Is Ending

O Lord,
you have been with me all through the day.
Now evening has come.
The shadows have lengthened into darkness.
Let my busy world grow quiet,
the feverish concerns of my day be stilled,
my work put away.

It was not today that I finally gave you
my whole attention
and saw and felt how sweet you are.
When shall I finally give you all of myself?

I beseech you Lord that the yearnings of my heart
and my deepest desires

may move you,
and that you will incline your ear to hear my prayers.

Grant me now a moment of your silence.
Keep me in your embrace through the night,
give me quiet rest
and your peace,
now and forever.
Amen.

Day Nineteen

My Day Begins

My Jesus,
the light and brightness of everlasting glory,
the joy of all Christian people
walking and laboring as pilgrims
in the wilderness of this world!
My heart cries out to you without words,
but my silence speaks to you and says:
How long must I wait for you, my Lord, to come?
Truly I trust that you will soon come to me,

your poorest servant,
and comfort me and make me joyous and glad in you,
delivering me from all anguish and sorrow.

Come O Lord, come,
for without you I have no glad day nor hour.
You are all my joy and gladness,
and without you my soul is barren and empty.
I am a prisoner bound with fetters until you,
through the light of your presence,
visit me, refresh me, and bring again to me
the liberty of spirit.
Show your face to me.
Let others seek what they will,
but truly there is nothing that I will seek
nothing that shall please me.

You my Lord are
my health and everlasting life.

I will not stop praying that you will come to me.

Speak to my spirit and say:
I am here.
I have come to you
because you have called me.
Your meekness and your sorrow
have brought me to you.

And I shall say again:
Lord I have called you and have desired to have you.
I am ready to forsake all things for you (3:31).

All Through the Day

I am here.

My Day Is Ending

O Lord,
you have been with me all through the day.
Now evening has come.
The shadows have lengthened into darkness.
Let my busy world grow quiet,
the feverish concerns of my day be stilled,
my work put away.

In the silence of the night say to me:
I am here.
I have come to you
because you have called upon me.
And I shall say again:

"Lord I have called you and desired to have you.
I am ready to forsake
all things for you."

Grant me a moment of your silence.
Keep me in your embrace through the night,
give me quiet rest
and your peace,
now and forever.
Amen.

Day Twenty

•••••

My Day Begins

My friend, says the Lord Jesus,
I said to my disciples:
My peace I leave with you, my peace I give you,
not as the world gives,
but much more than it may give.

All men desire peace, but not all are willing to do
that which leads to peace.
My peace is with the meek and mild in heart.

With those who demonstrate much patience.
If you will hear me and follow my words,
you shall know great peace.

O Lord what shall I do to experience this peace?

You shall in everything you do
watch carefully what you say and do,
and you shall intend always to please me
and you shall desire nothing but me.
You shall not judge others presumptuously
or meddle with things that do not concern you.
If you do this you shall be little troubled.
But not ever to feel at any time some kind of trouble,
heaviness of body and soul,
is not to be expected in this life,

but only in the life to come.

Do not believe that you have found true peace
when you feel no sorrow,
nor that all is well with you when you have no enemy,
nor that all is perfect
when you have everything your heart desires,
nor that you are especially beloved of God
just because prayer comes easily.
For a true lover of virtue is not known by these things,
and true peace is not built on them.

My peace comes to those
who offer their heart wholly to God (3:25).

All Through the Day

It is one thing to desire peace,
it is another to do what leads to peace.

My Day Is Ending

O Lord,
you have been with me all through the day.
Now evening has come.
The shadows have lengthened into darkness.
Let my busy world grow quiet,
the feverish concerns of my day be stilled,
my work put away.

You have promised us peace, O Lord,
not as the world promises,
but as only you can promise.
Grant me that peace.
But grant me also the patience and the courage
to do whatever your peace requires of me.

Remind me daily that your peace comes only to those
who offer their heart wholly to you.

Grant me a moment of your silence.
Keep me in your embrace through the night,
give me quiet rest
and your peace,
now and forever.
Amen.

Day Twenty-One

My Day Begins

My friend,
give all for all,
abandon your self-love.
For the love of yourself is more hurtful to your spirit
than any other thing in this world.

Desire nothing that is not lawful for you to have.
Keep nothing that may hinder your spiritual journey
or strip you of your spiritual freedom.

The passing things of this world,
even when we have many of them,
do not help us to find peace,
but only when we see them for what they are
and remove them from the love and desire of our heart.
This is true not just of our love of gold and silver
and other worldly riches,
but of our need and desire for honor and praise.
All these things vanish quickly
like smoke in the wind.

Ask yourself:
Why am I eaten up with vain sorrow?
Why am I wearied with superfluous cares?
Observe my will
and you shall find nothing

that will hurt or hinder you.
But if you seek this or that,
or to be in this place or that
just for your own sake and profit,
you shall never be at rest
and your soul shall never be free of troubles,
for in every place
you will find something to disturb you.
Nothing will give you peace
unless your spirit is grounded in me (3:27).

All Through the Day

The riches of this world vanish quickly,
like smoke in the wind.

My Day Is Ending

O Lord,
you have been with me all through the day.
Now evening has come.
The shadows have lengthened into darkness.
Let my busy world grow quiet,
the feverish concerns of my day be stilled,
my work put away.

Even as the day passes quickly
so do all the things of this world,
not just gold and silver,
but my need for honor and praise.
None of them lead to your promised peace.

I shall never be at peace
as long as I seek them.
I shall never know rest
until my hope is grounded in you.

Grant me a moment of your silence.
Keep me in your embrace through the night,
give me quiet rest
and your peace,
now and forever.
Amen.

Day Twenty-Two

◆◆◆◆◆

My Day Begins

Strengthen me, O Lord,
by the grace of the Holy Spirit,
and give me grace to be spiritually strong
and to rid my soul of all unimportant business
of the world and of the flesh
that I may not be led by shifting desires
for what the world promises.

Grant that I may see all things of the world
as they truly are—transitory and short abiding.

Let me see myself in the same light.
For nothing under the sun shall last forever.
And wise is the one who feels and understands
this to be true.

Therefore Lord, give me true heavenly wisdom that
I may learn to seek you and to find you,
and above all things to love you,
and to see all else
according to your wisdom and never otherwise.

Grant me the grace
to stay away from those who flatter me,
and to show patience to those that hurt me.
For it is great wisdom
not to be moved with every blast of hurtful words,
or by every warm breath of flattery.

Our peace cannot be built on the opinions of others.

Where then is true peace and glory?
Only in our Lord.
Therefore if we neither desire to please others
nor dread displeasing them,
we shall know the great peace we seek.

From wrongly placed faith and empty fears
come all unquietness of heart
and restlessness of soul (3:27/28).

All Through the Day

Nothing under the sun
lasts forever.

My Day Is Ending

O Lord,
you have been with me all through the day.
Now evening has come.
The shadows have lengthened into darkness.
Let my busy world grow quiet,
the feverish concerns of my day be stilled,
my work put away.

Grant me as the day ends the wisdom
to see the world as it truly is—
transitory and short-lived,
and to see myself in the same light.
Nothing under the sun lasts forever,

and true wisdom is in knowing this to be true.
Let me be wise enough to seek only you
and above all things to love only you.

Grant me a moment of your silence.
Keep me in your embrace through the night,
give me quiet rest and
your peace,
now and forever.
Amen.

Day Twenty-Three

My Day Begins

My friend,
I am the Lord who will send you comfort
in your times of trouble.
Come to me therefore
when all is not well with you.

What hinders you most is
that you are slow to turn to me.
Before you pray to me in earnest,
you seek your answer in the things of the world.

And all your efforts bring little comfort.

You must remember that
I am the source of all comfort
to those who call on me,
and that without me
there is no real comfort or remedy
for your suffering.

Take heart,
turn to me for comfort
and put your whole trust in my mercy.
For I am near you to help you
and to restore you to grace,
in even greater abundance
than you have ever known.

Is there anything hard or impossible to me?
Am I like those who say they will help and do nothing?
Where is your faith?
Stand strongly with me and persevere in me.
Be steadfast, abiding my promise,
and you shall have comfort
in such time as will be best for you.
Be patient my friend, be patient,
and wait for me.
I shall come soon to you and help you (3:30).

All Through the Day

Be patient, my friend, be patient
and I will come to you.

My Day Is Ending

O Lord,
you have been with me all through the day.
Now evening has come.
The shadows have lengthened into darkness.
Let my busy world grow quiet,
the feverish concerns of my day be stilled,
my work put away.

It is a time for patience.
I must remember
that you are the source of comfort
for all those who call on you,
and that without you
there is no real comfort in our times of trouble.

Let me never forget that you are always near.
Let me take heart and turn to you
and put my whole trust in your mercy.

Grant me a moment of your silence.
Keep me in your embrace through the night,
give me quiet rest
and your peace,
now and forever.
Amen.

Day Twenty-Four

My Day Begins

It is temptation that worries you,
and vague dread of the future that makes you afraid.
But to what avail is this fear and dread
about things that may never happen?
Your spiritual enemies desire that
you should pile fear upon sorrow.
Be patient with your present troubles, therefore,
and do not overly fear those that might come,
for the evil of today is enough.

It is a vain thing and spiritually unprofitable
to be either sad or glad about things
that may never happen.
It is human instability that leaves you open
to the suggestions of the evil one
who doesn't care whether he deceives you
with truth or falsity,
by love of things present or fear of things to come.

Therefore be not troubled and fear not.
Trust firmly in me and in my mercy have perfect hope.
For when you think that you are far from me,
often I am closest to you
and when you think all is lost,
often times your greatest rewards are closest to hand.

You are not lost when things go wrong.

Do not take any sorrows so seriously
that you lose your confidence in me.

I said to my disciples:
As my Father loves me, I love you.
And yet I sent them forth into the world
not to have passing joys but to wage great battles;
not to be honored, but to be looked down upon;
not to be idle, but to labor;
not to rest, but to bring forth much good fruit
in patience and in good works.

My friend,
remember well these words that I have spoken to you,
they are true and cannot be denied (3:31).

All Through the Day

As my Father loves me,
I love you.

My Day Is Ending

O Lord,
you have been with me all through the day.
Now evening has come.
The shadows have lengthened into darkness.
Let my busy world grow quiet,
the feverish concerns of my day be stilled,
my work put away.

Remind me often
that when I think you are far from me
you may be the closest.
When I think all is lost,
your greatest graces are often closest to hand.
I am not lost when things go wrong.

Let me not take my troubles so seriously
that I lose my trust in you,
for as your father loves you, you love me.

Grant me a moment of your silence.
Keep me in your embrace through the night,
give me quiet rest
and your peace,
now and forever.
Amen.

Day Twenty-Five

My Day Begins

Who shall give me wings like a dove
that I might fly into
the arms of my savior
and rest there?

I can see that no one is more at rest
than the person whose mind and heart
is always directed upward to God
with no desire for the things of this world.

Those who want to find you and behold you
must rise above all creatures, especially themselves.
If they are to behold you and see
that you are one alone
and that nothing on earth is like you,
they must free themselves from the love of all creatures.
They must be attentive to God alone.

To contemplate God requires a great grace
because it is meant to lift our soul far beyond itself.
For unless we are lifted up in spirit above ourselves
and clearly freed from a love of any creature
and perfectly united to God,
whatever we have or know,
whatever our virtues or learning,
is of little account.

It is often asked
whether one is rich, strong, fair, able,
a good writer, a good singer, or a good laborer.
But it is seldom asked whether that person
is poor in spirit, patient, meek, devout,
or inwardly turned to God.
The world judges by appearances
but we must look to the Spirit.

The world is often deceived,
but if we put all our trust in God
we are never deceived (3:31).

All Through the Day

The world judges by appearances
but I must look to the Spirit.

My Day Is Ending

O Lord,
you have been with me all through the day.
Now evening has come.
The shadows have lengthened into darkness.
Let my busy world grow quiet,
the feverish concerns of my day be stilled,
my work put away.

To keep the eye of my soul on you, Lord,
requires an abundance of your grace.
For I need to be lifted in spirit above myself
and freed from my love for created things.
Grant me this grace,

for I do understand
that no one is more at rest
than the person whose heart is directed
upwards to you.

Grant me a moment of your silence.
Keep me in your embrace through the night,
give me quiet rest
and your peace,
now and forever.
Amen.

Day Twenty-Six

◆◆◆◆◆

My Day Begins

My Lord God is to me all in all!
What more could I have?
What more could I desire?
How sweet and fulfilling this sounds,
but only to someone who loves the Word
and not the world.

To someone who understands it is enough to say this,
but I wish to speak even more plainly and say:
Lord when you are present all things are pleasant

and loving,
but when you are absent
all things are sad and unlovable.
When you come to me
you put my heart at rest
and fill it with new joy.
Let me so love you
that I understand the truth about you.
You grant me true judgment in all things,
and in all things I praise and adore you.

O Lord, without you
nothing stays pleasant for long,
for if anything is lovable,
it is only through the help of your grace
and the depth of your wisdom.

O everlasting light,
far surpassing everything that has been made,
send down beams of your light from above
and purify, gladden, and illumine
the innermost parts of my heart.
Quicken my spirit with all the powers thereof,
that it may cleave fast and be joined to you
in joyful gladness of spiritual love.
O when shall that blessed hour come
when you will visit me
and gladden me with your blessed presence,
so that you will truly be my all in all?
As long as that gift is not given me,
there shall be in my spirit
no full joy (3:35).

All Through the Day

My Lord God, be to me all in all.

My Day Is Ending

O Lord,
you have been with me all through the day.
Now evening has come.
The shadows have lengthened into darkness.
Let my busy world grow quiet,
the feverish concerns of my day be stilled,
my work put away.

Day after day Lord I discover again
that when you are present
everything is pleasing and lovable,
but when I feel your absence
everything is sad and unlovable.
Be present to me always, my Lord,

put my heart at rest
restore joy to my days.

Grant me a moment of your silence.
Keep me in your embrace through the night,
give me quiet rest
and your peace,
now and forever.
Amen.

Day Twenty-Seven

◆◆◆◆◆

My Day Begins

My friend, says the Lord,
commit your life to me
and I shall dispose of it well for you
when the time shall come.
Keep my laws, listen to my direction,
and you will find great profit and help.

O Lord, gladly will I put all things in your keeping
because I can do little for myself.
I wish I did not cling so strongly to worldly things

but instead offered myself wholly to you
and to your pleasure.

My friend,
the temptation is to trust only
in yourself and your own will
to bring about what you desire.
But often when you get what you desire
you feel differently about it.
For human affections often go in many directions,
driving a person from one thing to the next.
It is, however, no small thing for someone
to fully forsake one's own will even in small things.

Truly the perfection of a person is in perfect self-denial.
Such a person is truly free and loved by God.
But our old enemies resist our turn to goodness

in every way,
and hour after hour assault us to see
if they can catch us unaware.

Therefore stay awake,
and pray that you be not turned
from your spiritual goals
by temptation (3:49).

All Through the Day

It is no small thing
to forsake one's will
even in small things.

My Day Is Ending

O Lord,
you have been with me all through the day.
Now evening has come.
The shadows have lengthened into darkness.
Let my busy world grow quiet,
the feverish concerns of my day be stilled,
my work put away.

Let me put all things in your safe keeping
because I can do so little for myself.
I wish I did not cling so strongly to earthly values,
but could offer myself wholly to you.
I know my happiness is in perfect self-denial,

only then am I perfectly free.
But it is no small thing to let go of myself
even in very small things.

Grant me a moment of your silence.
Keep me in your embrace through the night,
give me quiet rest
and your peace,
now and forever.
Amen.

Day Twenty-Eight

My Day Begins

My Lord, pardon me,
and mercifully forgive me,
when during prayer my mind wanders from you.
Many times I am not here in your presence,
not where I stand or sit,
but rather I am wherever my thoughts lead me.
I hear you, everlasting truth, saying to me:
Where your treasure is, there is your heart.
If I love what is spiritual

I will speak gladly of spiritual things,
and of those things that pertain to God,
glorifying and worshipping his holy name.
If I love the world, I take my joy in its pleasures.
If I love the flesh, I imagine its joys.
But if I love that which is spiritual,
I take my joy in speaking of its worth.
I speak gladly of whatever I love
and bear it in my soul easily.

Blessed are they
who for the sake of the Lord
forget the things of this world
and learn truly to overcome themselves,
so that with a pure and clean conscience
they may offer their prayers to you.

Blessed are they who are worthy
of the company of angels.

Send me the light of your grace
and break down in me all that is not of you.

Send me your love and break the power of evil over me.
Center in you all the powers of my soul.
Help me, you who are everlasting truth,
to overcome any hold that vanity has over me.
Instill in me your heavenly sweetness
and overcome in me
every lingering trace of sin's bitterness (3:48).

All Through the Day

Where my treasure is,
there is my heart.

My Day Is Ending

O Lord,
you have been with me all through the day.
Now evening has come.
The shadows have lengthened into darkness.
Let my busy world grow quiet,
the feverish concerns of my day be stilled,
my work put away.

Always I find it so difficult to stay in your presence.
I go wherever my thoughts lead me,
and I hear you reminding me,
where my treasure is, there is my heart.

Center my heart and soul and mind in you.
Send me the light of your grace.
Remind me that you are present to me always,
and that you alone are my treasure.

Grant me a moment of your silence.
Keep me in your embrace through the night,
give me quiet rest
and your peace,
now and forever.
Amen.

Day Twenty-Nine

My Day Begins

My Lord, why do I continue
to place my trust in this world,
why do I expect my consolation to be here and now?
Is it not you my Lord whose mercy is without measure?
When has it ever been well for me without your grace?
And when was it not well for me
when you were present to me?
I had rather be poor with you
than rich without you.

Where you are is heaven;
where you are not is death and hell.

You are all I desire.
I have nothing to trust in but you.
You are my hope, my trust, my comfort,
and you are my most faithful friend
in every need.
Bless and make holy my soul
with your heavenly blessings,
that my spirit may be your dwelling place
and the seat of your glory.
Let nothing be found in me at any time
to offend your majesty.
To trust in you above all things
is the only comfort your servants desire.

198

To you, therefore, the Father of mercy,
do I lift up my eyes.
In you, only my Lord God,
do I put my trust.

Behold me, Lord,
and in your great goodness and generous mercy
graciously hear my prayer.

Defend and keep me
and through your grace direct me
into the ways of peace
and everlasting truth
without end (3:59).

All Through the Day

You are my most faithful friend
in every need.

My Day Is Ending

O Lord,
you have been with me all through the day.
Now evening has come.
The shadows have lengthened into darkness.
Let my busy world grow quiet,
the feverish concerns of my day be stilled,
my work put away.

Let it be true when I say
that you Lord are all I desire.
For truly I have nothing to trust in but you.
You are my hope, my trust, my comfort,
and you are my most faithful friend in every need.

Bless and make holy my spirit
with your gifts of grace.
Make my soul your dwelling place.
Hear my prayers.

Grant me a moment of your silence.
Keep me in your embrace through the night,
give me quiet rest
and your peace,
now and forever.
Amen.

Day Thirty

My Day Begins

My friend, says the Lord,
do not be overwhelmed by impatience
with the labor you have undertaken for my sake,
nor allow sorrow to cast you into despair,
nor into any unreasonable anguish or heaviness of heart.
Be comforted and strengthened by my promises,
for I have the power to reward you
and my other servants abundantly,
beyond what you could ever imagine.

You shall not labor here forever
or be burdened with a heavy heart.
Trust my promises
and you shall soon see an end to all your troubles.
An hour is coming
when all your troubles and labors will cease.
And truly that hour is at hand
for all is short that is measured in time.

My peace will come to you one day
and that day will never end.
You will know steadfast peace
and secure rest without end.
You shall not ever again say:
"Deliver me from the body of death."
For death shall be destroyed

and health of body and soul will be yours forever.
You shall never again know uneasiness of spirit
but only blessed joy.

Lift up your heart therefore to heaven
and see how I and all my saints who are with me now
knew great struggle while we were on earth.
Now they have everlasting joy and comfort in me.

Come,
abide with me in the kingdom of my Father,
without end (3:47).

All Through the Day

An hour is coming
when all your troubles and labors
will cease.

My Day Is Ending

O Lord,
you have been with me all through the day.
Now evening has come.
The shadows have lengthened into darkness.
Let my busy world grow quiet,
the feverish concerns of my day be stilled,
my work put away.

I know an hour is coming
when all my troubles and labors will cease,
and I know that hour is at hand,
for everything about this world passes quickly.

Your peace will come to me one day soon
and that peace will never end.
I will know your peace
and secure rest without end.

Grant me now a moment of your silence.
Keep me in your embrace through the night,
give me quiet rest
and your peace,
now and forever.
Amen.

One Final Word

This book was created to be nothing more than a gateway—a gateway to the spiritual wisdom of a specific teacher, and a gateway opening on your own spiritual path.

You may decide that Thomas á Kempis is someone whose experience of God is one that you wish to follow more closely and deeply. In that case you should get a copy of the entire text of *The Imitation of Christ* and pray it as you have prayed this gateway journey.

You may decide that his experience has not helped you. There are many other teachers. Somewhere there is the right teacher for your own, very special, absolutely unique journey of the spirit. You *will* find your teacher, you *will* discover your path.

We would not be searching, as St. Augustine reminds us, if we had not already found.